survival

Dona Herweck Rice

Consultant

Sterling Vamvas
Chemist, Orange County
Water District

Image Credits: Cover & p.1 iStock; p. 20–21 (background) Anthony Pierce/Alamy; pp.22 (bottom), 24–25 (background) blickwinkel/Alamy; p.20 Marvin Dembinsky Photo Associates/Alamy; p.23 (top) Juniors Bildarchiv GmbH/Alamy; p.25 (bottom) The Natural History Museum/Alamy; p.21 (bottom) Steve Bloom Images/Alamy; p.15 (illustration) Tim Bradley; p.19 (top) Joel Sartore/Getty Images; p.17 (middle) Lexa Hoang; backcover & pp.2–5 (background & bottom right), 6–7 (background), 9–12 (top), 13 (bottom), 14 (top right), 16–17 (background & bottom left), 17–18 (background), 22 (top), 25–26 (background) iStock; p.32 Megan Iatzko; p.8 (bottom right) Cordelia Molloy/Science Source; p.8 (top left) NOAA Okeanos Explorer Program, INDEX-SATAL 2010, NOAA/OER; p.17 (top) Power and Syred/SPL/Science Source; p.23 (bottom) Wikipedia; p.18 (bottom left) Art Wolfe/Science Source; pp.28–29 (illustrations) Janelle Bell-Martin; all other images from Shutterstock.

Library of Congress Cataloging-in-Publication Data

Rice, Dona, author.
  Traits for survival / Dona Herweck Rice.
    pages cm
  Summary: "Some animals are covered in fuzzy fur. Others travel thousands of miles each year, searching for warm weather and food. Some can even blend into their environment. These are traits that help animals survive"—Provided by publisher.
  Audience: K to grade 3.
  Includes index.
  ISBN 978-1-4807-4639-8 (pbk.)
  ISBN 1-4807-4639-8 (pbk.)
  ISBN 978-1-4807-5083-8 (ebook)
  1. Animals—Adaptation—Juvenile literature.
  2. Animal defenses—Juvenile literature.
  3. Adaptation (Biology)—Juvenile literature. I. Title.
  QH546.R54 2015
  591.47—dc23
                                    2014034230

Teacher Created Materials

5301 Oceanus Drive
Huntington Beach, CA 92649-1030
http://www.tcmpub.com

ISBN 978-1-4807-4639-8

Table of Contents

What a Life!

Where on Earth would you like to live? Chances are, you can find a way to live there! Do you want to live in a blazing hot desert? Houses built underground or with a good air conditioner can help you live comfortably in the heat. Do you want to live under the sea? A watertight house with air piped in can make that happen. How about living in a freezing **tundra**? Thick walls and a good parka can help make that possible.

king penguins

We humans can deal with the conditions of almost any place we want to live. We have amazing brains that make a lot of things possible for us. But what if we *couldn't* use our brains to help us survive the conditions of our **environment**? Our bodies would have to **adapt** to make life livable.

clown frogfish

boreal owl

Adaptation is the name of the game for animal **species**. Qualities that offer the best chance for survival grow strongest in a species. Qualities that don't support its chances fade away—or the species does!

Species hold on to what makes them best able to survive. Of course, a species doesn't just think, "Hey, this is working out pretty well for us. Let's keep it!" It doesn't choose anything. Instead, an animal's body adapts over time.

But sudden changes may come to a species' home. A drought may stop the flow of water. Food sources could die out. Or fire may destroy a species' home. Species don't adapt quickly to such big changes. They need to move to a new home, or they may die out.

Dogs don't sweat through their skin like humans do. They have adapted to pant, which circulates air in their bodies and cools them down.

Five Fierce Senses

Species rely on their senses of taste, touch, hearing, smelling, and seeing to survive.

Hearing

Whales communicate with one another across thousands of miles of ocean water.

Sight

Owls that need to spot their **prey** from great distances have developed sharp eyesight.

Smell

Sharks have adapted to smell and locate a single drop of blood.

Taste

Humans have developed a dislike for foods that taste bitter, as these foods are sometimes poisonous.

Touch

Plants like the Venus flytrap have sensitive leaves that feel when a tasty meal has landed on them.

Power Traits

Traits are the qualities that exist in DNA. There are physical traits such as eye color and the shape of teeth. And there are **instincts**, such as the urge to hunt or mate.

Among these traits are traits for survival. These are the qualities that help a species live and **thrive**. Many of them are adaptations. They help species adapt to fit their environment. These adaptations may change over time to give species the best chance to survive. Without these traits, many species would have died out long ago.

Some traits are common, and you may know them well. But some traits are uncommon—and as weird as anything you can imagine!

Cats' bodies have adapted to make them great hunters. Their eyes give them night vision to hunt their prey in the dark.

Tripod Fish

The tripod fish has adapted for fast-food dining! The fish's body has bony spikes that anchor it to the ocean floor. It faces the oncoming current with its mouth open, and food just floats down the hatch!

DNA

Information about a body's traits is in its cells. That's where DNA is. DNA tells the body everything from what color to grow your hair to how to eat food. Every living creature has DNA.

skin color

DNA

eye color

hair color

The Family That Lives Together...Lives

Have you noticed how some **animals** live in groups? Whether they live in packs, flocks, or families, they work together. Why? Survival!

There is safety in numbers! The bigger the group, the less chance they will be attacked. It also means they can help one another if an attack does come. Best of all, there is always someone on the watch for **predators**!

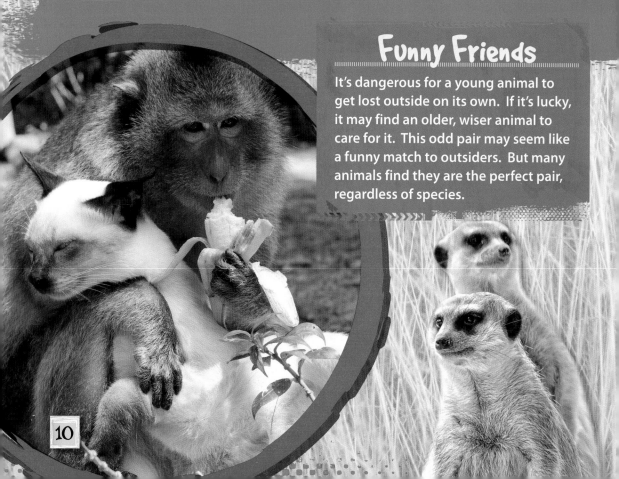

Funny Friends

It's dangerous for a young animal to get lost outside on its own. If it's lucky, it may find an older, wiser animal to care for it. This odd pair may seem like a funny match to outsiders. But many animals find they are the perfect pair, regardless of species.

Big numbers also mean that there are more animals to find food. For example, a pack of wolves can surround and kill prey easier than a lone, or single, wolf can. And a group of animals can work together to find nuts and grains for all.

Another advantage to living in a group is that there are always others to care for the young. If a few animals watch after the young, it allows others in the group to perform other jobs that are needed.

Meerkats live in a group called a *mob*.

More Is More

Here are a few of the males and females that work together to care for their young:

- giant water bugs
- poison-arrow frogs
- deer mice
- penguins
- red foxes
- meerkats

Moving On!

Animals move for one reason: to survive. Some animals move every year. They move from one type of **climate** to another. Or they move to follow food or to find a mate. They often move home again when the weather warms or the food returns. This movement is called **migration**.

Migration is a survival trait. It allows animals to go where they need to in order to live well. If animals had a trait that told them to stay in one place and the species could not survive the change of seasons, the species would eventually die out. Instead, many animals have adapted and know to migrate. This ensures the species will live.

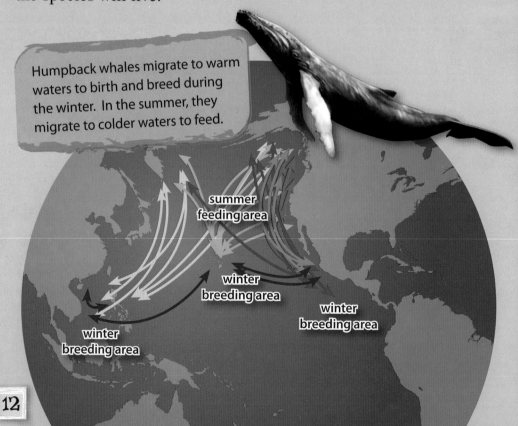

Humpback whales migrate to warm waters to birth and breed during the winter. In the summer, they migrate to colder waters to feed.

summer feeding area

winter breeding area

winter breeding area

winter breeding area

Micro-Migrations

Some migrations take years to complete. Others take only a day. The jellyfish in Palau's Jellyfish Lake float from east to west every day—just like the sun.

The Arctic tern, a type of bird, migrates every year from the Arctic to Antarctica—a round-trip distance of more than 32,000 kilometers (20,000 miles)!

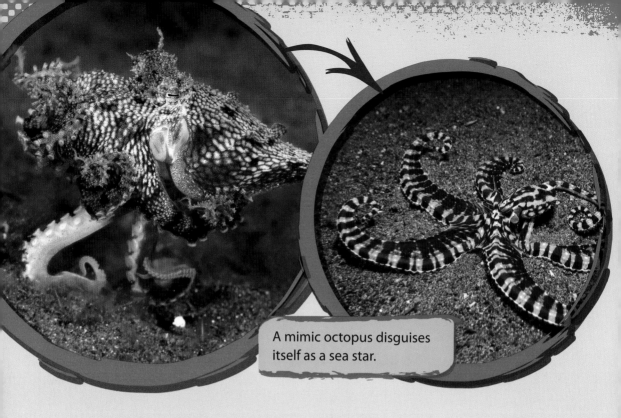

A mimic octopus disguises itself as a sea star.

You Can't See Me!

What do you do when you don't want to be recognized? You wear a disguise! In a way, some animals wear them, too. They have an adaptation that makes them difficult to see. It's called *camouflage*. Camouflage allows them to blend into their surroundings. This makes it tough for predators to spot them.

There are many types of camouflage. The walking stick insect looks just like a twig. The wings of a caligo butterfly look like the eyes of an owl. Owls can look like tree trunks, and toads can look like leaves. Some animals even change their skin color or shape to blend in. For example, all octopuses can change their skin color. But the mimic octopus can make itself look like at least 15 different underwater creatures!

"Who me? I'm just a little meerkat like you. Nothing to worry about here."

Tricked Ya!

The drongo bird uses sounds as a form of camouflage. It can make the calls of around 50 different species. It uses its special talent to get animals to abandon their food. Then, it swoops in and chows down.

Mimicry is a type of camouflage used by animals who want to look dangerous to scare away predators.

Hairy Beast

We humans love our hair! We wash it, brush it, cut it, and style it. We wear it every way we can think of. But animals don't think about how their hair looks. They need their hair . . . for survival!

Hair, or fur, gives animals protection and warmth. The musk ox is a great example. Its hair is thick and shaggy. It grows long to completely cover the musk ox's body. That helps the musk ox stay warm in the freezing tundra where it lives.

Caribou also have amazing fur. They have two layers of hair covering their skin. The fur closest to the skin is frizzy and crinkly, and the hair on top is thick and hollow. The hollow hair acts like **insulation** to keep in the caribou's body heat.

musk ox

Unlike human hair, whiskers can be used by cats to feel things.

Hollow Hairs

Polar bears have thick fur to keep them warm in their cold Arctic environment. Each hair is hollow, which provides extra insulation. This hair acts as a wet suit for polar bears.

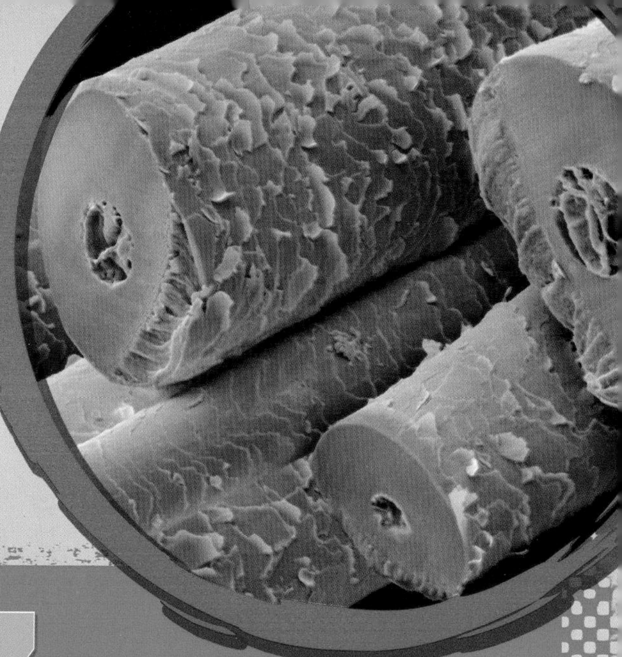

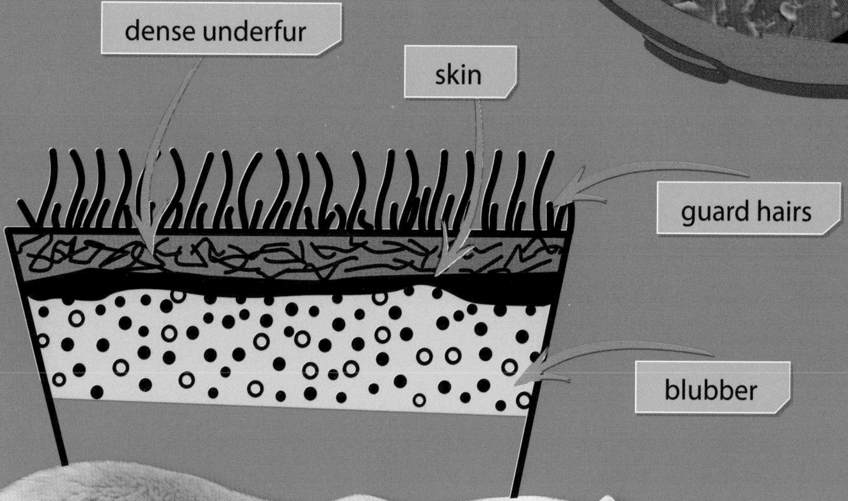

dense underfur

skin

guard hairs

blubber

Super Skin!

A polar bear has a thick layer of blubber to stay warm. The skin beneath its fur is black because the dark color holds in heat best. It also has two layers of fur for extra warmth.

Hold On!

Most of us can't last too long unless there's a store nearby. And we need our kitchen sink for a glass of water. But some animals have adapted to live in places with little food and water.

The Bactrian (BAK-tree-uhn) camel's body is about as perfect as it can get when it comes to survival. It lives with deep freezes in winter and blazing heat in summer. Its two humps are loaded with fat. The fat can be used for energy or water. In fact, the camel can live a full week without drinking and months without eating!

What a Face!

Camels have thick eyebrows to block the hot sun, long eyelashes to protect their eyes from sandstorms, and nostrils that can open and close like eyelids to block out blowing sand.

Gentlemen, We Can Rebuild Him

Some animals can regenerate, or grow new limbs. Some lizards can do this, and sea stars can, too. Talk about an amazing adaptation!

Bactrian camels save water by not sweating until temperatures reach about 41° Celsius (105° Fahrenheit).

I Can Fly

Humans have found a way to fly with machines. But many animals have adapted for flight naturally. Planes? Who needs them!

Why is flight a great trait for survival? It helps animals get away from predators fast! It also helps some predators go after prey even faster. And when food is scarce, a flying animal can get a good bird's-eye view. It can spot its next meal from high above in the sky.

Flight goes hand in hand with another adaptation. Most flying animals have super lung power! Flying takes a lot more energy than running does. About one-fifth of a bird's body is used to breathe. Humans only use about one-twentieth of their bodies to breathe.

Nighty Night

In areas with harsh winters, some animals sleep for months! Actually, they **hibernate** to conserve energy. This adaptation makes everything in an animal's body slow down, and they seem to be in a deep, deep sleep.

It's a Bird. ~~It's a Plane.~~
It's a Fish!

Flying fish jump out of the water to escape predators. They simply spread their fins and fly through the air.

flying fish

A flying squirrel doesn't have flying power. It glides. Adaptations to its skin let it catch the air just right to glide between trees.

Soooo BIG!

puffer fish

Little kids like to play the So Big game, making themselves as big as they can be. For many animals, So Big is an adaptation that helps them survive. When faced with a threat, their instincts kick in. They make themselves seem larger than they are.

One of the weirdest examples of this is the puffer fish. When it gets scared, it takes in air or water in a special sac in its body. Then, it blows up like a balloon. It only takes a few seconds to do this! It can let out the air and water pretty quickly, too, and go back to its normal size.

The frilled lizard and cobra use size as a warning, too. The frilled lizard flares its frill, and the cobra flares its hood. The flare is its way of saying, "I'm warning you. Back off!"

A frilled lizard eats its prey.

How to Scare a Bear

If you are out in the woods and see a bear, keep your distance. But if you can't avoid the bear, use what you know about adaptations to help you.

1. Make a lot of noise.
2. Stand with your friends and family to make your group look more threatening.
3. Spread your arms over your head to appear as large as possible.

Definitely Not Bambi

Deer are cute and sweet, right? Not the tufted deer. It has an unusual adaptation—fangs! The male uses its fangs to fight other males for a mate. If one deer knocks down the other, its fangs will finish the job.

Licked!

The okapi uses its foot-long tongue to grab leaves from plants. But it can also clean its own eyeballs and ears with its long, muscular tongue. Eww!

When a bird uses another bird to raise its young, it is called a *brood parasite*.

It's You or Me, Kid!

Many parents care for their young in the animal world. They keep their young safe so they can grow up and have more young. That is how the species lives on.

But that's not true for everyone! Some animals survive by having other animals raise their young. It's strange but true.

Many types of cuckoo (KOO-koo) birds lay their eggs in other birds' nests. The other birds hatch and raise the cuckoo babies. The cuckoo babies are often bigger and tougher than the other birds in the nest. They may even kill the other babies!

This works out great for the cuckoo. The cuckoo's babies are raised without any trouble to the cuckoo. And the baby gets rid of other birds that would compete for its food and space.

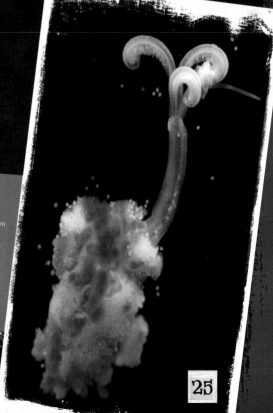

Zombie Worm

The aptly named zombie worm has no mouth. It oozes acid from its body onto its food. The food becomes liquid, and the worm sucks it in through its skin. It can "eat" meat and even bones this way!

Survivor!

Why all this fuss about traits for survival? What's the big deal about adaptation? Survival is key in the animal world. Traits that give a species the best chance to survive are the traits that last. Traits that don't are the ones that die out. They die out, or the species does.

The small elephant hawk moth outsmarts its predators by looking like a leaf on this tree.

To live and thrive, a species needs strong survival traits. And over time, those traits change. No one can predict exactly what the future will be like. So, the most successful species might be the most flexible. And flexibility is one trait that humans have!

Adaptations happen very slowly over time.

They may even take thousands of years!

Think Like a Scientist

How does the shape of a bird's beak affect what it eats? Experiment and find out!

What to Get

- forks
- mini marshmallows
- plastic cups
- spoons
- straws
- timer
- toothpicks
- tweezers

What to Do

1 In groups of four, have each person grab a plastic cup. Then, have each person choose a fork, a spoon, a straw, or tweezers.

2 Pour a pile of toothpicks on the floor. Set the timer for 40 seconds. When the timer starts, use your tool to pick up as many toothpicks as you can. Record the results on a chart like the one below.

	Fork	Spoon	Straw	Tweezers
Toothpicks				
Marshmallows				

3 Repeat step two. This time, use mini marshmallows instead of toothpicks.

4 Which beaks, or tools, worked the best? Which did not work very well? Create a bar graph to show your results. What does this tell you about the shape of a bird's beak?

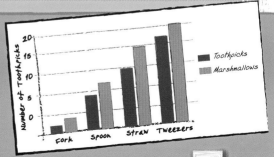

Glossary

adapt—to change so that it is easier to live in a particular place

climate—the usual type of weather a place gets

environment—the natural world

hibernate—to spend the winter sleeping or resting

instincts—ways of behaving, thinking, or feeling that are not learned

insulation—a material or substance that is used to stop heat from going in or out of something

migration—the act of moving from one area to another at different times of the year

predators—animals that live by killing and eating other animals

prey—animals that are hunted by other animals for food

species—groups of animals or plants that are similar and can produce young animals or plants

thrive—to grow and develop successfully

traits—qualities that make living things different from one another

tundra—a large area of flat land where there are no trees and the ground is always frozen

Index

Your Turn!

My eyes help me see.

My nose helps me smell.

My hair keeps my head warm.

My teeth help me chew.

Amazing You

Take a good long look at yourself in the mirror. What traits do you notice that give you special abilities to survive? Also, think about what you can't see. What traits do you have inside that help you survive and thrive? Design a poster for your room that shows your amazing traits for survival.

5